FIGHTING FOR CUBA! FIGHTING FOR SOCIALISM!

AND OTHER SPEECHES
BY MIGUEL DÍAZ-CANEL BERMÚDEZ

First published in October 2023 by
1804 Books, New York, NY
1804Books.com
This selection © 1804 Books, New York, NY

ISBN: 979-8-9882602-4-0
Library of Congress Control Number: 2024934981

Cover by Vivek Venkatraman

TABLE OF CONTENTS

Foreword	v
Editor's Note	xi
Speeches	
We Are More! And We Will Win!	1
What is Urgently Needed is the Political Will to Truly 'Leave No One Behind'	13
Long Live the Friendship between Our Peoples!	17
We Will Never Give Up the Right to Defend Ourselves!	23
Fighting for Cuba! Fighting for Socialism!	33
Biographies	41

FOREWORD

THE VOICE OF THE SOUTH, THE VOICE OF CUBA, IN NEW YORK

On Sunday, September 17, President Miguel Díaz-Canel Bermúdez arrived in New York City. Minutes before boarding the plane in Havana, he had announced in his X profile that he would be at the United Nations. The rumor about his possible visit had been going around for weeks, between campaigns to prevent it on the one hand, and preparations to receive him on the other: love and hate at its maximum expression, as almost always when it comes to the Caribbean island.

"Cuba will be there, representing the claims of the Summit of the Group of 77 and China, and the claims of our people," he wrote shortly before leaving the homeland. The stay in New York would last seven days, from Sunday to Sunday, during which he did not have a minute of rest.

Havana had just hosted a Summit of the G-77 and China, the largest and most diverse group in the multilateral sphere, with 134 member states, which undoubtedly renewed the work of this important force of Southern countries. Cuba had assumed its presidency for the first time earlier this year.

Heads of state, prime ministers, foreign ministers, ministers of the Global South—in short, more than a hundred delegations had gathered in Cuba to discuss the role of Science, Technology, and Innovation, an issue that the island has historically led, with special emphasis under the presidency of Díaz-Canel.

The President went from one battle to another in less than twenty-four hours. It was not by chance that the president's first activity was to meet with Cuban diplomats as soon as he set foot in the city that never sleeps. "What we did was a heroic deed," he told them, between fatigue and emotion. "To have convened a summit of this magnitude at the present time, in the midst of the world situation, and on the eve of the United Nations General Assembly session to be held here, was a great challenge."

There in 315 Lexington Avenue, the headquarters of Cuba's Permanent Mission to the UN, Díaz-Canel foresaw that the days ahead would be quite complex, "but we come with the decision that the country is going to achieve a diplomatic and political victory." Whoever thinks that Cuba is isolated, said the president, their arguments have collapsed.

He was talking about the backing given by the Havana Summit and also about the upcoming days that the Cuban delegation would experience. Díaz-Canel would be at the United Nations on behalf of Cuba, but also, and above all, on behalf of the countries of the South; represented in his voice would be, one by one, each of the struggles and demands of the always neglected.

He also carried on his shoulders a moving history marked by the four visits of Commander-in-Chief Fidel Castro Ruz to that international forum (in 1960, 1979, 1995, and 2000); and that of Army General Raúl Castro Ruz in 2015, when the triumph of December 17, 2014 was still fresh: the day that President Obama recognized that the blockade against Cuba had been a failure and the tenacity of the Cuban people turned into a victory. Now Díaz-Canel arrived once again, with a blockade that goes beyond cruelty and that, as he himself has said, has tried to take away even our oxygen.

This time in his first three days at the United Nations—let's remember that September 2018 was his inaugural visit to this, shall we say, "frenetic" space of world diplomacy—he participated in four summits or high-level meetings: on the Sustainable Development

Goals; on Climate Ambition; on Pandemic Prevention, Preparedness, and Response; as well as Financing for Development.

The most important day was September 19 when the General Debate began, and President Díaz-Canel was the sixth speaker to take the floor—a privileged place, experts say, because it occurred on the first morning of a six-day discussion in which 189 heads of delegations spoke; Niger, Madagascar, Afghanistan, and Myanmar were the only UN member states that did not take the podium of the green-hued marbles.

Before Díaz-Canel, Lula and Biden spoke (Brazil and the United States always come first and second by tradition); so did the representatives of Colombia, Jordan, and Poland. A detail that went unnoticed: the Cuban leader, displaying his courtesy, courage, and infinite patience, stayed to listen to Biden's speech, who spoke of how "with concerted leadership and careful effort, adversaries can become partners, overwhelming challenges can be resolved and deep wounds can heal." He was referring to Vietnam, a country in which the United States caused more than one million deaths in war. He did not speak of Cuba, for according to Biden, in his endless double standard, "there are adversaries and adversaries."

In the most important speech of his days in New York, the head of state said that he was bringing "to this assembly the voice of the South, the voice of the exploited and vilified, as Che Guevara was heard to say in this very hall almost sixty years ago." Díaz-Canel spoke on behalf of the G-77 and denounced the enormous inequalities between a minority of highly developed nations and a majority that cannot overcome the euphemism of "developing nations."

"We are not asking for handouts or begging for favors," said the President of the G-77. He said that we are claiming our rights and demanding a profound transformation of the current international financial architecture, "because it is profoundly unjust, anachronistic, and dysfunctional; because it was designed to profit from the reserves of the South."

The president strongly criticized "unilateral coercive measures, euphemistically called sanctions, which have become the practice of powerful states that pretend to act as universal judges." He spoke of Cuba, fustigated like few others, but also of Venezuela, Nicaragua, Zimbabwe, Syria, the Democratic People's Republic of Korea and Iran. With his voice he raised the solidarity with the cause of the Palestinian people and the right to self-determination of the Saharawi people.

Díaz-Canel denounced the viciousness and surgical precision with which Washington and Florida have calculated the way to inflict the greatest possible damage to Cuban families. He spoke about the more-than-sixty years of suffering Cuba has experienced under the oppressive economic blockade and denounced before the UN how the US government pressured entities not to supply the medical oxygen and pulmonary ventilators needed on the island to face the pandemic peak.

"Our scientists created the vaccines and developed the pulmonary ventilators that saved the country and that we made available to other countries in the world!" said the President of Cuba, that nation that resists suffocation and creates.

It was also that country of shadows and lights that Díaz-Canel showed to all those who were interested in meeting with him during those days in New York: businessmen; leaders of various Christian denominations; science and technology professionals, also from the US public health system; managers, representatives, artists, and cultural promoters; Cuban immigrants. Respect, love for the island, eagerness to work together, and rejection of the blockade prevailed in all of them. There were also doubts about Cuba, which, as the President said in his statements upon his return to the island, were clarified.

An extremely moving moment of those days in the Big Apple was, without the slightest doubt, the visit to the Malcolm X & Dr. Betty Shabazz Memorial and Educational Center. "You cannot imagine," the statesman confessed to those who waited for him there, "how much emotion we Cubans feel as we visit you here today to pay homage to Malcolm X, and I believe we are also paying homage to Fidel."

Díaz-Canel described that moment as "one of the most extraordinary experiences we are going to have in life," when he also recalled that he belonged to a generation of Cubans who "grew up reading and hearing about Malcolm X":

> He was one of the true heroes of this country that the Cuban Revolution taught us to respect and love, precisely when in other parts of the world, at that time, the American hero was Clark Kent, better known as Superman, and contradictorily the fighters for civil rights suffered harassment, persecution, defamation and silence.

"Malcolm X and Fidel would be happy to have a moment like this," African-American activist and writer Rosemarie Mealy told the press. Mealy is the author of *Fidel & Malcolm X: Memories of a Meeting*, a book about that unique and historic meeting between the Cuban leader and the US civil rights fighter at the Hotel Theresa in Harlem.

Díaz-Canel's visit took place a few hours before the sixty-third anniversary of that meeting, which added magic to Díaz-Canel's first time in that neighborhood which once embraced and took good care of Fidel and others intended to boycott his presence at the United Nations. It was 1960.

More than six decades later, the Cuban president, son of that generation of bearded men who landed in New York, was retracing the steps of the Commander-in-Chief Fidel Castro. And he did so with the merit of continuing the Revolution forged by the heroes of his childhood and youth, under other fires, as intense as those that melted in more than half a century the work born on January 1, 1959.

That is why Díaz-Canel was embraced in New York. And in that embrace were the people who gathered on the corner of Lexington and Thirty-Eighth Street, whom he went to thank in the middle of the street to the astonishment of all, amidst a tremendous uproar, amidst his personal escorts and those other senior men of the US Secret Service, whose faces could be read with stupefaction.

That happened the day before the final embrace, when more than eight hundred people—many of them young faces marked by the legacy of the Cuban Revolution—gathered in a heartfelt act of solidarity to tell Cuba that it is not alone, that it is an example for the world, that its classification as a State Sponsor of Terrorism is an aberration and a shameless act, and that the struggle at its side continues. Two Molotov cocktails thrown at the Cuban embassy in Washington just a few hours later were the negative reaction to that diplomatic and political victory announced by Díaz-Canel as soon as he arrived in New York.

As a friend and colleague wrote that last night in the city: "someday it will be told in all the corners of the world, with justice, what Cuba in revolution has been, how much love it has had and has to give, and how dearly the unfading dream of turning this, our world, into a home closer to humanity has cost us." May the following pages help in that purpose. Cuba needs it, and is grateful.

Leticia Martínez Hernández
Havana, October 3, 2023

EDITOR'S NOTE

Enclosed in the following pages are five speeches given in September 2023 by Cuban president Miguel Díaz-Canel Bermudez at the Group of 77 and China (G-77 and China) Summit in Havana and during his historic trip to New York later that month. The G-77 and China represents over 80 percent of the world's population—a striking majority, many of whom live in developing countries choked by neocolonial and neoliberal economic policies. With Cuba at its helm for 2023, the G-77 and China met in Havana leading up to the UN General Assembly (UNGA) and immediately made clear its objective: to fight for a just and sustainable system that preserves the lives and dignity of people in the Global South. Knowing the stakes of this moment, this objective becomes only more prescient. The planet is increasingly at risk of destruction from climate change, and the first to feel its effects are impoverished people around the world as well as those in developing countries.

It is with this urgency we publish the following speeches from President Miguel Díaz-Canel. First the inaugural meeting of the G-77 and China in Havana elaborates on the unjust nature of the climate crisis, as those who contribute the most to its acceleration will feel its consequences last. This speech sets the stage for the address that follows, delivered at the Summit of the Sustainable Development Goals. These seventeen goals were set in 2015 to be completed by 2030, but at this moment they are unlikely to be achieved due to negligence of Western powers. Later that day, the president visited the Malcolm X & Dr. Betty Shabazz Memorial and Educational Center, and spoke to the historic ties between oppressed peoples in the United States and those who fought for freedom in Cuba. These themes come together as Díaz-Canel addresses the UNGA: he underscores the need for a new system that prioritizes sustainability, sovereignty, and solidarity, as well as reiterates the call for normal relations with the US. As it stands, the country is still under siege from the sixty-year blockade and its unjust place on the State Sponsors of Terrorism list (SSOT), both of which bar the country from essential resources and infrastructure. And this call is echoed by thousands within the US. In the final speech, he meets organizers from all over the country who are fighting for an end to US imperialism's stranglehold on the island, speaking to the resistance that the Cuban people have taken up, as well as the importance of solidarity with the US.

This solidarity resonates across the world: last year, the UN passed a resolution condemning the blockade on Cuba for the thirtieth time. As usual, the only countries that voted against it were the United States and Israel. The ongoing Let Cuba Live campaign is an international call for solidarity with the island, a stand against the blockade, the SSOT list, and all attempts to thwart the sovereignty of the Cuban people. Today, a historic campaign is in motion to get one million signatures to demand US president Joe Biden remove the island from the SSOT list. From social organizations and leaders, popular movements, faith-based movements; to artists, athletes, journalists, peace associations, and all those in defense of human rights and equality—the call to Let Cuba Live can be heard worldwide!

These speeches and exchanges represent the continued solidarity that the world expresses, not just out of a kindness for the Cuban people, but also for an understanding that a new world order is necessary for the survival and dignity of all peoples and the planet. It is with this solidarity that we share and uplift the words of President Díaz-Canel in this booklet, and it is with this feeling we cry: we will overcome!

SPEECHES

SEPTEMBER 15, 2023

WE ARE MORE! AND WE WILL WIN!

Speech delivered at the Inaugural Session of the Summit of Heads of State and Government of the Group of 77 and China, on the Current Challenges of Development: Role of Science, Technology and Innovation at the Convention Palace in Havana, Cuba

Excellencies;
Distinguished delegates and guests:

You are all warmly welcome to Cuba, the land of José Martí, to whom we owe the beautiful idea that homeland is humanity.

Thank you for accepting the invitation that unites us today in defense of the future of the great majorities that make up the bulk of that great and unifying concept that is humanity.

As announced by the Cuban Foreign Minister on the eve of the Summit, this is an austere summit, and I hope you will excuse any shortcomings you may encounter. Cuba is literally encircled by a six-decade blockade and by all the difficulties that derive from that siege, which are now reinforced. We also face, of course, the colossal challenges that are a consequence of the current unjust international order—but we are not the only ones. Almost sixty years ago, it was the communion of difficulties and the hope that together we could face and overcome them that brought us into being as a group. We are the 77 and China! And we are more!

As you will experience during these days, we lack many things, but we have plenty of feelings: friendship, solidarity, and brotherhood. And we have more than enough will to make you feel like family. You are all at home! You can also be assured that we will do our utmost to ensure that our deliberations lead to tangible results, in a climate of solidarity and cooperation that makes the collective mission possible.

The Group of 77 and China has the immense responsibility of representing the interests of the majority of the nations of the planet on the international stage. For historical and identity reasons, we keep the original name, but we are more, much more than 77 countries. Today we are 135, equivalent to more than two-thirds of the member states of the United Nations (UN), where 80 percent of the world's population lives. Meeting at the summit level gives us the opportunity to deliberate collectively and, at the highest political level, to join forces in defense of the interests of these majorities. It helps us to reconcile positions in the face of current challenges to the development and well-being of our peoples. But it also raises questions.

After almost sixty years of diplomatic battles, in the difficult and, to this day, very unsuccessful attempt to transform the unjust and anachronistic rules that govern international economic relations, it is worth remembering the calls of our historic leaders to democratize the United Nations Organization: the warnings of Fidel Castro that "tomorrow will be too late," and the unforgettable phrase of Comandante Hugo Chávez, when he said that we presidents go from "summit to summit" and the people from "abyss to abyss." The Bolivarian leader advocated for meetings that were truly useful, from which concrete benefits could emerge for the people awaiting solutions, who are on the brink of the same abyss into which we have been plunged by the selfishness of those who have been cutting the cake for centuries and leaving us with the leftovers.

This summit is taking place at a time when humanity has reached a scientific and technical potential unimaginable a couple of decades ago, one with an extraordinary capacity to generate wealth and well-being that, under conditions of greater equality, equity, and justice, could ensure decent, comfortable, and sustainable standards of living for almost all the inhabitants of the planet. If we color the space occupied by the member nations of the Group on a world map, we will see two forces that no one can overcome. We are more and we are more diverse! "The South also exists," say the verses of the Uruguayan poet Mario Benedetti. For all the time that the North has accommodated the world to its interests to the detriment of the rest, it is now up to the South to change the rules of the game.

"It is the hour of the ovens, in which nothing but light is to be seen," José Martí would say. And he is right: the vast majority of the members of the Group of 77—the main victims of the current multidimensional crisis affecting the world, of the cyclical imbalances in international trade and finance, of the abusive unequal exchange, of the scientific, technological, and knowledge gap, of the effects of climate change, and of the danger of progressive destruction and depletion of the natural resources on which life on the planet depends—we demand the pending democratization of the system of international relations.

It is the peoples of the South who suffer most from poverty, hunger, misery, deaths from curable diseases, illiteracy, human displacement, and other consequences of underdevelopment. Many of our nations are called poor, when in fact they should be considered impoverished nations. And it is necessary to reverse this condition into which centuries of colonial and neocolonial dependence have plunged us, because it is not fair and because the South can no longer bear the dead weight of all these misfortunes. Those who built dazzling cities with the resources, sweat, and blood of the nations of the South are already suffering, and will suffer more in the future, from the consequences of the economic and social imbalances caused by the plundering because we travel on the same ship, although some are VIP passengers and others their servants. The only valid way for this "world-ship" not to end up like the Titanic is cooperation, solidarity, the African philosophy of Ubuntu, which understands human progress without exclusions, where the pain and hope of each one is the pain and hope of all.

Excellencies:

We have proposed the role of science, technology, and innovation as the theme of this summit, and as essential components of the political debate associated with development. We do so convinced that it is the achievements and progress in this field that will ultimately tell if and when it is possible to achieve the Sustainable Development Goals related to the end of poverty, to zero hunger in the world, to health and well-being, quality education, gender equality, clean water and sanitation, to solutions to the problems of energy, labor, economic growth, industrialization, and social justice. I am absolutely convinced that it will be impossible to advance towards a sustainable way of life, in harmony with the natural conditions that guarantee life on the planet, without these premises. And it is obvious that a transformative process towards the achievement of these objectives contemplates, in one way or another, the role of knowledge as a generator of science, technology, and innovation.

The international barriers, that have hindered access to knowledge by developing countries and their use of factors that are so crucial for economic and social progress, must now be broken down. I am talking about barriers intimately associated with an unjust and unsustainable international economic order that perpetuates conditions of privilege for developed countries and relegates the majority of humanity to conditions of underdevelopment. Without addressing these issues, the sustainable development to which we are all entitled cannot be achieved in any way, no matter how many goals are set. Nor will it be possible to narrow the immense gap that separates the privileged living conditions of a small segment of the planet's population from the underdevelopment that is deepening among the great majorities. Nor can we be confident that we will achieve a world of peace, in which wars and armed conflicts of all kinds will disappear.

Science, technology, and innovation play a transcendental role in promoting productivity, efficiency, creating added value, humanizing working conditions, boosting well-being, and ensuring human development. We are facing the greatest scientific-technical revolution humanity has ever known. Science has modified the very course of life. Human beings have been able to know outer space and devise sophisticated machines that automate even the most elementary processes associated with their existence. The internet has erased spatial and temporal limits. Technological development has made it possible to connect the world and eliminate thousands of kilometers of distance at the speed of a click. It has multiplied teaching and learning capabilities, accelerated research processes, and endowed the human race with unsuspected capacities to improve their living conditions. But these possibilities are not within everyone's reach.

In this regard, the United Nations Industrial Development Organization (UNIDO) has highlighted that the creation and diffusion of advanced digital production technologies (ADP) remains concentrated at the global level, with very weak development in most economies of the South. Only ten economies—leaders in ADP technologies—are responsible for 90 percent of all patents worldwide and 70 percent of the total exports are directly related to them. Far from becoming tools to close the development gap and contribute to overcoming the injustices that threaten the very destiny of humanity, these technologies tend to become weapons to deepen that gap, bending the will of many governments and protecting the system of exploitation and plunder that for several centuries has nurtured the wealth of the former colonial powers and relegated our nations to a subordinate role.

This explains why, in the midst of the most colossal scientific and technical development of all times, the world has gone back three decades in terms of reducing extreme poverty, and there are levels of famine not seen since 2005. It explains why in the South more than 84 million children remain out of school and more than 600 million people are without electricity; why only 36 percent of the population uses the internet in the least developed countries and landlocked developing nations, compared to 92 percent with access in developed countries. Consider that the average cost of a smartphone barely represents

2 percent of monthly per capita income in North America, while this figure rises to 53 percent in South Asia and 39 percent in sub-Saharan Africa. There can be no serious talk of technological progress or equitable access to communications in the face of these realities.

The energy transition is also taking place in conditions of profound inequality, which tend to perpetuate itself. The disproportion in energy consumption between developed countries—167.9 gigajoules per person per year—and developing countries—56.2 gigajoules per person per year—is a consequence of the existing economic and social gap and is also the reason why this gap will continue to widen. Per capita electricity consumption in OECD [Organisation for Economic Co-operation and Development] countries is 2.38 times higher than the world average and 16 times higher than in Sub-Saharan Africa.

A substantial proportion of the diseases most prevalent in developing countries are those that are preventable and/or treatable. The World Health Organization stated in its World Health Report that an estimated eight million people die prematurely each year from preventable diseases and conditions. These deaths account for approximately one-third of all human deaths worldwide each year.

We have a duty to try to change the rules of the game and we will only succeed if we mobilize joint action.

All, or almost all of us, try to attract foreign direct investment as a necessary component of our development and management of our economies. Sometimes we achieve the objective that this should be accompanied by some transfer of technology. But we know that most often it is not accompanied by the transfer of knowledge and capacity-building assistance. This absence leads to developing countries being placed in the lowest links of global value chains, and their research in health, food, environment, and other areas is either very limited or systematically devalued.

This phenomenon occurs alongside the talent drain, or what is commonly referred to as "brain drain," i.e., the practice of more developed countries benefiting from the training and knowledge of professionals whom developing countries painstakingly train, often without any support from wealthier nations. This is a massive drain and a remarkable financial contribution made by the developing countries to the rich ones; much greater, by the way, than Official Development Assistance, evident from the migratory flow that is devastating for the underdeveloped countries.

Another reality is the tendency to patent everything. This is a practice that increases the coffers of large transnational corporations in the most powerful countries and makes the remaining economies more fragile. Thus, the rampant process of privatization of information contributes to widening the knowledge gap and limits access to development. There is pressure on developing countries to introduce laws to protect intellectual property rights, and it is deliberately forgotten that many industrialized countries became developed precisely by pirating products and technologies outside their geographical borders, especially in what are now developing countries.

Patent applications continued to increase, even in the midst of the pandemic, in 2020, by 1.5 percent, and soared in 2021, growing by 3.6 percent. Health-related technologies continued to record the fastest growth among all sectors. During 2021, trademark applications reached 3.4 million worldwide, increasing 5.5 percent over 2020. However, it was uneven by region: Asia received two thirds, 67.6 percent, of all applications filed driven mainly by growth in China; North America, 18.5 percent. While Europe with 10.5 percent; Africa, 0.6 percent; Latin America and the Caribbean, 1.6 percent; and Oceania, 0.6 percent accounted for the lowest percentages of all applications.

The gender gap in innovation persists. The number of personnel dedicated to research increased at a rate three times faster—13.7 percent—than the growth of the world's population—4.6 percent—in the period 2014–2018. However, only one-third of researchers are women. According to the World Intellectual Property Organization, men still represent a large majority of people associated with patented inventions in the world. Only 17 percent of the persons designated as inventors in international patent applications were women in 2021.

The privatization of knowledge limits its circulation and recombination. It poses limitations to progress and scientific solutions to problems. It constitutes a significant barrier to development and the role that science, technology, and innovation should play in it. It aggravates socioeconomic conditions in developing countries.

Suffice it to say that in the midst of the greatest pandemic humanity has ever known, only ten manufacturers accounted for 70 percent of the production of vaccines against COVID-19. The pandemic made starkly evident the cost of scientific and digital exclusion, which claimed lives and widened the gap between the North and the South. As a result, developing countries had only 24 doses of vaccines per 100 inhabitants, while the richest countries had almost 150 doses per 100 people. In the face of the call to multiply solidarity and put aside disagreements, the world ended up being absurdly more selfish.

The World Health Organization has formulated the well-known "10/90 gap," according to which 90 percent of health research resources are devoted to diseases that account for 10 percent of mortality and morbidity, while those that account for 90 percent of mortality and morbidity have only 10 percent of the resources. In the aftermath of the pandemic, our countries have had to go through extremely complex circumstances, from which they are still struggling to get back on their feet.

When turning to the financial markets, the nations of the South have faced interest rates up to eight times higher than those of developed countries. About one-fifth of developing economies liquidated more than 15 percent of their international foreign exchange reserves to cushion the pressure on national currencies. In 2022, twenty-five developing nations had to devote more than one-fifth of their total income to servicing public external debt, which amounts to a new form of exploitation.

Global spending on research and development increased by 19.2 percent between 2014 and 2018, outpacing the growth rate of the world economy of 14.6 percent. However, it remains highly concentrated, with 93 percent being contributed by the G20 countries. The resources needed for a fundamental solution to these problems exist. In 2022 alone, global military spending reached a record $2.24 trillion, or trillions of dollars. How much could be done with these resources for the benefit of the South? Achieving universal and inclusive participation in the digital economy will require at least $428 billion to be invested in our countries by 2030, a demand that can be met with just 19 percent of global military spending.

However, the South seems destined to live on the crumbs that the current system has reserved for it. The International Monetary Fund's financial support to the least developed and other low-income countries, from 2020 to the end of November 2022, is less than what the Coca-Cola Company has spent on brand advertising alone over the last eight years. Meanwhile, less than 2 percent of the already deficient Official Development Assistance has been dedicated to science, technology, and innovation capacities. Estimates indicate that 9 percent of global military spending could finance climate change adaptation in ten years, and 7 percent would be sufficient to cover the cost of universal pandemic vaccination.

An international financial architecture that perpetuates such disparities and forces the South to tie up financial resources and go into debt to protect itself from the instability that the system itself generates, that enlarges the pockets of the rich at the expense of the reserves of the poorest 80 percent, is undoubtedly an architecture hostile to the progress of our nations. It must be demolished if we really aspire to work for the development of the great mass of nations gathered here.

Excellencies:

It must be a priority task to overthrow, once and for all, the research paradigms that are limited to the cultural environments and perspectives of the North, and which deprive the international scientific community of considerable intellectual capital. This trend poses a premise for our nations: the urgency of rescuing confidence in the most dynamic element of our societies: the human being and his creative activity.

In this endeavor, capacity building is key to realizing the promise of science, technology, and innovation for sustainable development. In this regard, we recognize the merit of the Global Development Initiative, promoted by the president of the People's Republic of China, Xi Jinping. It is an inclusive proposal, consistent with the need for a new just and equitable international order, which places knowledge-based development where it belongs: at the center of the priorities of the international system.

Even though Cuba is a developing country burdened by great economic difficulties, it has scientific capabilities that should not be underestimated and that are part of the legacy of the historic leader of the Cuban Revolution, Commander in Chief Fidel Castro Ruz, who, with a vision of the future, identified a source of development in this field. We have a government management system based on science and innovation, which has become an important strength for the preservation of our sovereignty, with its best expression in the creation of Cuba's own vaccines against COVID-19.

However, for Cuba, connecting knowledge with the solution of development problems is a gigantic task, because these efforts must take place in the midst of an iron economic, commercial, and financial blockade that results in significant resource limitations. To cite just one example: by policy decision of the US government, many web sites dedicated to knowledge and science are specifically blocked to Cuban researchers.

This is not the place to expand on the impact that the criminal economic blockade of the United States has on our economy, our scientific-technical progress, and our development, with a humanitarian cost that becomes visible. But I must identify it as a fundamental obstacle, in spite of which Cuba has had the capacity to achieve indisputable results in science and innovation on the basis of an iron political will.

During these days, I invite you to discuss the challenges of the development of our nations, the injustices that keep us from global progress, but also the value of our unity and our rich store of knowledge. Let us direct our reflections to the search for consensus, strategies, tactics, and forms of coordination. Let us put on the table all our assets, let us enhance synergies. Let us show the value and expertise of the South in the face of those who present us as an amorphous mass in search of charity or assistance.

Let us remember that many of the unique nations represented by the Group of 77 and China wrote impressive pages of creativity and heroism in human history before colonization and plunder impoverished the destinies of a part of them. Let us recover that fighting spirit, traditional knowledge, creative thinking and collective wisdom. Let us fight for our right to development, which is also the right to exist as a species.

Only in this way will we be able to participate in the scientific-technical revolution on equal footing. Only in this way will we be able to occupy the place that belongs to us in this world, where today we are relegated to the condition of meek contributors of wealth for minorities. Let us fulfill together the honorable mission of completing this world, improving it, making it fairer and more rational, without the permanent threat of disappearing from our dreams.

Excellencies:

Twenty-three years ago, at a meeting like this one, the historic leader of the Cuban Revolution, Fidel Castro, stated:

> For the Group of 77, the present time cannot be one of pleading to the developed countries, nor of submission, defeatism or internal divisions, but of rescuing our spirit of struggle, of unity and cohesion around our demands.

We were promised fifty years ago that one day there would be no gap between developed and underdeveloped countries. We were promised bread and justice, and today there is less and less bread and less and less justice.

The validity of these words could be interpreted as a defeat of what this Group intended and has not been able to resolve. I ask you to take it as a confirmation of the long road we have traveled together and all the rights we have to demand the pending changes.

In homage to those who believed and founded, in the name of the peoples we represent, let us make their voices and claims respected!

We are more! And we will win!
Thank you very much.

SEPTEMBER 18, 2023

WHAT IS URGENTLY NEEDED IS THE POLITICAL WILL TO TRULY 'LEAVE NO ONE BEHIND'

Speech delivered at the Summit on Sustainable Development Goals in New York

Mr. President:

I have the honor to speak on behalf of the Group of 77 and China. The mid-term review of the 2030 Agenda for Sustainable Development is taking place at an extremely critical juncture, in which developing countries face multiple challenges and an unjust economic order that perpetuates inequalities and poverty. The reports produced by the Secretary-General contain irrefutable figures that reflect a rather grim reality. Even before the COVID-19 pandemic, the world was already off track towards achieving the Sustainable Development Goals (SDGs). We will reach 2030 with 575 million people living in extreme poverty. By that time, barely a third of the countries will succeed in halving national poverty levels. We will not eliminate hunger, as we had agreed. On the contrary, 735 million people currently suffer from chronic hunger, a figure higher than that recorded in 2015. At this rate, none of the 17 Sustainable Development Goals will be achieved, and more than half of the agreed targets will be missed.

Aware of the current situation, the Group of 77 and China have made this event a top priority, with the aim of putting sustainable development back at the center of the international agenda and providing the necessary political impetus to accelerate the implementation of the 2030 Agenda. It is in this spirit that the Group has embarked on the process of negotiating a political declaration in order to increase and accelerate the implementation of concrete, innovative, transformative, and ambitious actions and measures to ensure the achievement of the Sustainable Development Goals. It is in this context that the Group has spearheaded a global call for urgent reform of the international financial architecture, which has been shared by a large number of leaders and personalities from around the world. This call was broadly supported by the Secretary-General, who urged this Summit to correct the historical injustices that underlie the international financial system in order to provide the most vulnerable countries and people with better opportunities for a better future.

We must continue to defend the role of the General Assembly in the discussion if we are to ensure that the voice of every nation is heard and taken into account, as it should be, on such important issues relating to global governance.

This call also presupposes the existence of an improved global sovereign debt architecture with the participation of the South, making possible the application of a fair, balanced, and development-oriented treatment. The high cost of borrowing prevents developing countries from investing in the Sustainable Development Goals. Currently, twenty-five nations in the South spend more than 20 percent of their government revenues on debt service alone. At the same time, there is an urgent need for an early and substantial recapitalization of the Multilateral Development Banks so that they can radically improve their lending conditions and meet the financial needs of the South. In this regard, we urge the international community to follow up and support the Secretary-General's proposal for a "Sustainable Development Goals Stimulus" for developing countries, with the (objective) purpose of scaling up affordable long-term financing for development and aligning financial flows with the Sustainable Development Goals. We also urge developed countries to finally honor their unfulfilled Official Development Assistance commitments.

Excellencies:

The climate change agenda must be implemented in its entirety, in accordance with the United Nations Framework Convention on Climate Change and its Paris Agreement, upholding the principle of equality, and common but differentiated responsibilities and respective capabilities.

More ambitious targets in areas such as mitigation, adaptation, and the means to achieve them, as well as the delivery and mobilization of resources by developed countries are essential to combat climate change while addressing our development challenges. We strongly urge developed countries to fulfill their pledges in this area. Developing countries' efforts to implement the 2030 Agenda also need to be supported by concrete actions in terms of technology transfer and human resources training, as well as North-South cooperation, in order to foster industrialization and investments in quality, reliable, sustainable, and resilient infrastructure.

The international trading system must also be reformed, and sustainable supply chains must be created that will contribute to the achievement of the SDGs by promoting export-oriented economic growth in developing countries. To this end, special but differentiated treatment for developing countries should be strengthened as a multilateral principle. Unilateralism and protectionism, including unilateral protection and restrictions on trade, which are incompatible with the World Trade Organization Agreements, must be eliminated with utmost speed.

Such is the case of countries suffering from the imposition of unilateral coercive measures, which constitute a serious violation of the purposes and principles of the Charter of the United Nations. Such measures seriously hamper the efforts of the affected countries to achieve the SDGs and sustainable development in general. The international community, including the UN system, must continue to firmly reject the imposition of such measures and work for their unconditional elimination.

Excellencies:

The aforementioned claims have been stated on several occasions by the leaders of the South. The lack of progress should not be attributed to the absence of solutions. The actions are there. What is urgently needed is the political will to truly "leave no one behind" and overcome one of the most complex crises humanity has ever experienced in modern history. That would be our best contribution to the common future we need to build together!

Thank you very much.

SEPTEMBER 18, 2023

LONG LIVE THE FRIENDSHIP BETWEEN OUR PEOPLES!

Speech delivered at the Malcolm X & Dr. Betty Shabazz Memorial and Educational Center in New York

Dear friends, or better said, sisters and brothers:

You cannot imagine how much emotion we Cubans are feeling as we visit you here today to pay tribute to Malcolm, and I believe we are also paying tribute to Fidel.

Today we are commemorating an anniversary of a relationship that cemented the relations between the American people and the Cuban people. And because of the way in which that relationship was woven between Fidel and Malcolm, which was a relationship based on solidarity: when Fidel was denied his presence in a hotel in New York, Malcolm welcomed Fidel in solidarity and offered him the neighborhood of Harlem. And our common struggle today, of breaking the unjust blockade that the United States government has imposed on Cuba, is also a struggle to give continuity to that solidarity, that brotherhood, and that friendship that arose in the moment that we commemorate today, the meeting between Fidel and Malcolm X. In this battle of these times, we are also receiving the solidarity of the best of the American people. And when we defeat the blockade—and I am sure we are going to defeat it—that will be one of the best tributes to Malcolm, to Fidel, and to the relationship between the American people and the Cuban people.

You have been very wise when, in this place where Malcolm gave his last speech, you have conceived a center both to keep and preserve his memory, but also to be an educational center, because it is by educating in his ideas that the best tribute to Malcolm can be achieved. As I listened to you speaking before I took the floor, I was looking at those images [on the wall] that reflect the strength of Malcolm's action, that reinforce his ideas, that demonstrate his relationship with the American people, and his tireless struggle for social justice in the United States. And they have a lot to do with personal experiences that I have, but I am sure that my experiences can be shared in the same way by any of the members of our delegation, because almost all of us are from the same generation.

I remember when I was in the tenth grade, that is, the last grade of secondary education in Cuba at the time, an edition of *The Autobiography of Malcolm X* was published. Those of us who were young in Cuba ran to the bookstores to get it. It became one of those bedside books for young people at that age of rebellion. All of the images that are collected in that mural are in the text of that book. I remember that one of the things that amazed me the most, that impressed me the most when I read and studied the life of Malcolm X, was precisely how Malcolm X grew with his own actions, with his own political career; how in a self-taught way he began to study, to study in depth the most advanced ideas, to surpass himself. This allowed him to build such a strong ability to speak that, in a few years, he became one of the most impressive orators in the United States, an orator who, with the strength of his oratory, defended the cause of the poor, defended the causes of the oppressed, defended the cause of those who suffered most from racial discrimination in the United States. And so, Malcolm also became a paradigm of a revolutionary for young Cubans.

I believe that one of the most extraordinary experiences we are going to have in our lives will be this moment we are spending with you today, commemorating, remembering, but also thinking. Therefore, we thank you very much for giving us the opportunity to be here with you today, and we thank you from the bottom of our hearts for giving us the opportunity to be living this moment. As I have explained to you, we are from a generation of Cubans who grew up reading and hearing about Malcolm X. He was one of the true heroes of this country that the Cuban Revolution taught us to respect and love, precisely when in other parts of the world at that time the American hero was Clark Kent, better known as Superman, and contradictorily the fighters for civil rights suffered harassment, persecution, defamation, and silence.

In a recent tour of African nations, we reviewed the history of our common ancestors who came to America on the ships of slave traders. Slave traders who not only tore those human beings from their lands, their communities and their roots, who not only took away their freedom, which is like taking away our oxygen. They forced them to bear the names of those who appropriated their lives to exploit their labor force. They cut off, in the most brutal and humiliating way, one of the most sensitive legacies of any human being: their family. In that Malcolm X was also extremely singular and original. He was the one who first made us think of this dimension of the crime of slavery: with the X he added as his surname, he vindicated the unknown branch of his ancestry.

But that was not his only challenge to the system that, with racial segregation, gave continuity to the crime of trafficking in the United States. In his short and intense life—Malcolm lived thirty-nine years, just like Che Guevara—he broke all the molds imposed by the racist and segregationist narrative by becoming a keen observer of the social reality of his time and a radical activist in his environment. For Fidel and for Cuba he also defied the imperialist powers. The Cuban Revolution and the Cuban people will never forget his role in inviting the rebel leader and his delegation to stay at the Hotel Theresa, in the heart of the Black neighborhood of Harlem, when there was an attempt to boycott the Cuban presence at the United Nations in 1960. That generous and fraternal gesture culminated in the historic meeting between Malcolm X and Fidel in September 1960 and extended to the more discreet one with Che Guevara in 1964.

The violent death of the African-American leader who aroused so much sympathy among the revolutionaries of an era of hopeful revolutionary effervescence was, without a doubt, a hard blow for his family, especially for his wife Betty Shabazz and his daughters. It was a blow also to those who were inspired by his leadership, to those who were inspired by his eloquent words and his growing commitment to social justice. And it was a blow to his brothers in the struggle for ideals of justice around the world. For these and many other reasons that go without saying, we have come to honor Malcolm X and, with him, to pay tribute to our African-American brothers and sisters, to the people of the United States, to those who fight for justice and against exploitation and segregation, and to all who believe, as Malcolm and Fidel believed, that a better world is possible.

That biography of which I spoke at the beginning, which was published and widely disseminated in Cuba, showed us his firm commitment to social justice and his unconditional solidarity with the liberation movements of the African peoples. Malcolm X's intense activity as a fighter for the rights of the Afro-American people and the peoples of Africa, as well as his development as a revolutionary and his vertical behavior, led him to understand in the mature stage of his activism that the problem to be solved was not only racial or religious, but especially class-based, derived from an unjust and exclusive political and economic system.

In several speeches, we also heard Malcolm X mention the Cuban Revolution as an important and true referent of the struggle for justice of the people in their battle for freedom and independence. The Cuban delegation, which is in New York to attend the United Nations General Assembly, wanted to pay tribute to this place, where those who feared such a clear and committed vision of the destiny of the peoples violently cut short the lives of those who fought for independence. And because we are only a few blocks away, we also wanted to greet the community of the Harlem neighborhood, with which

Cubans have developed sentimental ties for many years and where Malcolm X deployed an important part of his political activism.

Let us all honor the memory and legacy of Malcolm X, as a commitment to those who have suffered and still suffer from poverty, injustice, and exclusion; to those who have suffered and still suffer as a consequence of colonialism, neocolonialism, imperialism, exploitation, racism, and selfishness.

That meeting between Malcolm X and Fidel Castro, that historic dialogue between them, which other generations of Cubans and Americans have held for more than six decades with mutual respect, admiration, and affection, is and will be the most beautiful proof of how much we, the children of both peoples who believe in justice and fight for it, have in common.

Long live the friendship between our peoples!
Long live Malcolm X!
Hasta la victoria siempre!

SEPTEMBER 19, 2023

WE WILL NEVER GIVE UP THE RIGHT TO DEFEND OURSELVES!

Speech delivered at the General Debate of the 78th Regular Session of the United Nations General Assembly in New York

Mr. President;
Mr. Secretary-General;
Excellencies:

I bring to this assembly the voice of the South, the voice of the "exploited and the vilified," as Che Guevara was heard saying in this very chamber almost sixty years ago.

We are a diverse peoples with common problems. We have just confirmed this in Havana, which was honored to host the summit of leaders and other high-level representatives of the Group of 77 and China, the most representative, broad, and diverse grouping of nations in the multilateral sphere. For two days, practically without a break, more than one hundred representatives of the 134 nations that make up the Group raised their voices to demand changes that can no longer be postponed in the unjust, irrational, and abusive international economic order, which has deepened, year after year, the enormous inequalities between a minority of highly developed nations and a majority that cannot overcome the euphemism of "developing nations."

Worse still, as the UN Secretary-General acknowledged at the Havana Summit, the G-77 was founded six decades ago to remedy centuries of injustice and neglect, and in today's troubled world its members are caught in a web of global crises where poverty is on the rise and hunger is increasing.

We were united by the need to change what has not been resolved and our condition as the main victims of the current multidimensional global crisis, of the abusive unequal exchange, of the scientific and technological gap, and of the degradation of the environment.

But we have also been united, for more than half a century, by the inescapable challenge and determination to transform the current international order which, in addition to being exclusive and irrational, is unsustainable for the planet and unviable for the well-being of all. The countries represented in the G-77 and China, where 80 percent of the world's population lives, not only have the challenge of development, but also the responsibility to modify the structures that marginalize us from global progress and turn many peoples of the South into laboratories for renewed forms of domination. A new and fairer global contract is urgently needed.

Mr. President:

Only seven years away from the deadline set for the hopeful 2030 Agenda, the outlook is discouraging. This august institution has already acknowledged it: at the current pace, none of the 17 Sustainable Development Goals will be achieved, and more than half of the 169 agreed targets will be missed.

In the twenty-first century, it offends the human condition that almost 800 million people suffer from hunger on a planet that produces enough to feed everyone. Or that in the age of knowledge and the accelerated development of information and communications technologies, more than 760 million people, two-thirds of them women, cannot read or write. The efforts of developing countries are not enough to implement the 2030 Agenda. They must be backed by concrete actions in terms of market access, financing on fair and preferential terms, technology transfer, and North-South cooperation.

We are not asking for handouts or begging for favors. The G-77 demands rights and will continue to demand a profound transformation of the current international financial architecture because it is profoundly unjust, anachronistic, and dysfunctional; because it was designed to profit from the reserves of the South, perpetuate a system of domination that increases underdevelopment, and reproduce a model of modern colonialism. We need and demand financial institutions in which our countries have real decision-making capacity and access to financing.

A recapitalization of the Multilateral Development Banks is urgently needed to radically improve their lending conditions and meet the financial needs of the South. The countries of this Group have had to allocate $379 billion of their reserves to defend their currencies in 2022, almost double the amount of new Special Drawing Rights allocated to them by the International Monetary Fund. It is necessary to rationalize, review, and change the role of credit rating agencies. It is also imperative to establish criteria that go beyond gross domestic product to define developing countries' access to concessional financing and adequate technical cooperation.

While the richest countries fail to meet their commitment to allocate at least 0.7 percent of their gross national product to Official Development Assistance, the nations of the South have to spend up to 14 percent of their income to pay interest on foreign debt. Most G-77 nations are forced to allocate more resources to debt service than to investments in health or education. What sustainable development can be achieved with such a noose around their necks?

The Group reiterates today its call to public, multilateral, and private creditors to refinance the debt through credit guarantees, lower interest rates, and longer maturities. We insist on the implementation of a multilateral mechanism for the renegotiation of sovereign debt with the effective participation of the countries of the South, allowing for fair, balanced, and development-oriented treatment. It is imperative to redesign debt instruments at once and include trigger clauses to provide relief and restructuring as soon as a country is affected by natural catastrophes or macroeconomic shocks—problems that are so common in the most vulnerable nations.

Mr. President:

No one sensible now disputes that climate change threatens the survival of all, with irreversible effects. Nor is it a secret that those who have the least influence on the climate crisis are those who suffer the most from its effects, in particular the Small Island Developing States. Meanwhile, the industrialized countries, voracious predators of resources and the environment, shirk their major responsibility and fail to meet their commitments under the Framework Convention on Climate Change and the Paris Agreement. To cite just one example, it is deeply disappointing that the target of mobilizing no less than $100 billion per year by 2020 as climate finance has never been met.

With a view to the 28th Conference of States Parties to the Framework Convention (COP28), priorities for the countries of the Group of 77 will be the Global Stocktaking exercise, the operationalization of the Loss and Damage Fund, the definition of the framework for the Adaptation Objective, and the establishment of a new climate finance target in full compliance with the principle of common but differentiated responsibilities.

The G-77 is convening a Southern Leaders' Summit to be held on December 2 in the context of COP28 in Dubai. This initiative, unprecedented in the framework of a Conference of the Parties, will be a space to articulate the positions of our Group at the highest level in the context of climate negotiations. COP28 will thus demonstrate, beyond the speeches, that there is real political will on the part of the developed nations to reach the agreements that cannot be postponed if they act in this way.

Mr. President:

A priority task for the G-77 is to change once and for all the paradigms of science, technology, and innovation which are limited to the environments and perspectives of the North, thus depriving the international scientific community of considerable intellectual capital.

The successful Summit in Havana launched an urgent call for the nucleation of science, technology, and innovation around the undeniable goal of sustainable development. There we decided to resume the work of the Consortium of Science, Technology, and Innovation for the South, in order to promote joint research projects and foster productive linkages to reduce dependence on Northern markets. We also agreed to promote the convening, by 2025, of a High-Level Meeting of the United Nations General Assembly on Science, Technology and Innovation for Development.

The seventeen cooperation projects that Cuba has set up in the framework of its presidency of the G-77 will contribute to channeling and triangulating the potential of South-South cooperation. We urge the richest nations and international organizations to participate in these initiatives.

Cuba will not relent in its efforts to boost the creative potential, influence, and leadership of the G-77. Our Group has much to contribute to multilateralism, stability, justice and rationality that the world requires today.

Excellencies:

To all the problems and challenges that characterize the reality of our nations and mobilize the peoples, we must add the use of unilateral coercive measures, euphemistically called "sanctions," which has become the practice of powerful states seeking to act as universal judges to weaken and destroy economies, and isolate and subjugate sovereign states.

Cuba is not the first sovereign state against which such measures have been launched, but it is the one that has endured them for the longest time, despite the worldwide condemnation that is expressed almost unanimously every year in this Assembly, and is disrespected and disregarded in this expressed will by the government of the world's largest economic, financial, and military power.

We were not the first and we are not the last. The pressures to isolate and weaken economies and sovereign states today also affect Venezuela, Nicaragua, and, before and after, have been the prelude to invasions and overthrow of "uncomfortable" governments in the Middle East. We reject the unilateral coercive measures imposed on countries such as Zimbabwe, Syria, the Democratic People's Republic of Korea, and Iran, among many other countries whose peoples suffer the negative impact of these measures.

We reiterate our solidarity with the cause of the Palestinian people. We support the right to self-determination of the Saharawi people. Let us fight for a world of peace without war and conflict!

Five years ago, I spoke for the first time from this podium, where the historic leader of the Cuban Revolution, Commander-in-Chief Fidel Castro Ruz, and Army General Raúl Castro Ruz have previously stood to expose those truths and ideals of peace and justice of a small archipelago that has resisted and will resist at the height of the dignity, courage, and unwavering firmness of its people and its history. But I cannot pass by this world platform without denouncing, once again, that for sixty years Cuba has been suffering from a suffocating economic blockade, designed to depress its income and standard of living, suffer continuous shortages of food, medicines, and other basic supplies, and limit its potential for development. That is the nature and those are the objectives of the policy of economic coercion and maximum pressure applied by the government of the United States against Cuba, in violation of International Law and the Charter of the United Nations.

There is not a single measure or action taken by Cuba to harm the United States, its economic sector, its commercial activity, or its social fabric. There is no act by Cuba that threatens the independence of the United States, its national security, impairs its sovereign rights, interferes in its internal affairs, or affects the welfare of its people. The nited States' conduct is absolutely unilateral and unjustified.

Every day, the Cuban people resist and creatively overcome these issues in the face of this ruthless economic war, which since 2019, during the full pandemic, has opportunistically escalated to an even more extreme, cruel, and inhuman dimension. The effects are brutal! The US government pressured entities from supplying the medical oxygen and pulmonary ventilators needed in Cuba to cope with the pandemic peak. Our Cuban scientists created the vaccines and developed the lung ventilators that saved the country and that we made available to other countries in the world!

With viciousness and surgical precision, Washington and Florida have calculated how to inflict the greatest possible damage on Cuban families. The United States is pursuing and has tried to prevent fuel and lubricant supplies to our country, an action that would seem unthinkable in peacetime. In a globalized world, it is not only absurd, but criminal, to prohibit access to technologies, including medical equipment, that have more than 10 percent US-made components. Its actions against the medical cooperation provided by Cuba in many nations are shameful. It goes so far as to openly threaten sovereign governments for requesting this contribution and responding to the public health needs of their populations.

The United States deprives its citizens of the right to travel to Cuba, in defiance of its own constitution. The tightening of the blockade has an impact on the high migratory flows registered in our country in recent years, which entails a painful cost for Cuban families and adverse demographic and economic consequences for the nation.

The United States government lies and does enormous damage to international efforts to combat terrorism when it accuses Cuba, without any basis whatsoever, of being a sponsor of that scourge. Under cover of this arbitrary and fraudulent accusation, they extort hundreds of banking and financial institutions around the world and force them to choose between continuing their relations with the United States or maintaining their ties with Cuba.

Our country is suffering a real siege, an extraterritorial, cruel, and silent economic war. This siege is accompanied by a powerful political machinery of destabilization, with millionaire funds approved by the US Congress, in order to capitalize on the shortages caused by the blockade and undermine the constitutional order of the country and the tranquility of the citizens.

Despite the hostility of your government, we will continue to build bridges with the people of the United States, as we do with all the peoples of the world. We will strengthen, more and more, the links with the Cuban emigration in any corner of the planet.

Mr. President:

The promotion and protection of human rights is a common ideal, which demands a genuine spirit of respect and constructive dialogue among states. Unfortunately, seventy-five years after the adoption of the Universal Declaration of Human Rights, the reality is very different. This issue [of coercive measures] has become a political weapon of powerful nations that seek to subject independent nations, mainly in the South, to their geopolitical designs. No country is exempt from challenges, just as no country has the authority to consider itself a paradigm in terms of human rights and stigmatize other models, cultures or sovereign states.

We defend dialogue and cooperation as effective ways for the promotion and protection of human rights, without politicization or selectivity, without the application of double standards, conditioning, or pressure. In this spirit, Cuba has presented its candidacy to the Human Rights Council for the period 2024 to 2026, in the elections to be held next October 10. We thank in advance the confidence of the countries that have already given us their valuable support. If elected, Cuba's voice will continue to be raised with a universal vision, always from the South, in favor of the legitimate interests of developing countries, from the constructive commitment and the unwavering responsibility for the full realization of all human rights for all.

Cuba will continue to strengthen its democracy and its socialist model, which, although under siege, has shown how much a small developing country with little natural wealth can do. We will continue our transformative process in the search for ways out of the siege imposed on us by US imperialism and for ways to achieve the prosperity with social justice that our people deserve.

In this endeavor, we will never give up the right to defend ourselves!

Mr. President;
Distinguished Heads of Delegation and other representatives:

I conclude by extending an invitation to all of us to work to overcome our differences and face common challenges together, with a sense of urgency. To this end, the United Nations and this General Assembly, even with their limitations, are the most powerful instrument at our disposal.

Always count on Cuba to defend multilateralism and to promote together peace and sustainable development for all!

It will always be an honor to fight for justice, sharing the difficulties and challenges with the peoples of the South, ready to change history! And we will win!

Thank you very much.

SEPTEMBER 23, 2023

FIGHTING FOR CUBA! FIGHTING FOR SOCIALISM!

Speech delivered at the Voices of Dignity Event in Solidarity with Cuba and Venezuela in New York

[*audience chants* "Cuba sí, bloqueo no! Cuba sí, bloqueo no!"]

Comrades;
Friends;
Sisters and brothers:

Cuba and Venezuela are certain that with the heroism of our peoples and your support, we will overcome!

We are very moved to participate in this act of solidarity from you, the dignified voices of the United States, the dignified voices of the American people who give enormous support to Cuba and Venezuela, to our sister revolutions by saying "NO" to sanctions and blockades.

Now I would like to ask you a question: after all that has been said here, after all the feelings that have been expressed, after you have heard a magnificent sample of American jazz music with the Latinity of Cuban music, by Maestro Arturo O'Farrill and his quintet, is it necessary for me to speak? [*audience exclamations of "Yes!"*] You are very kind and generous.

I have many things to express to you, feelings that come from the commitment to the revolutionary struggle of peoples like Venezuela, like Cuba, that when we see these demonstrations of solidarity, this commitment to support us, which you have proposed with dignified voices, one also feels an enormous commitment, because we know that we are not only fighting for Venezuela, we are not only fighting for Cuba, we are not only fighting for the countries and peoples of the South, but that you and all of us are fighting for a better world that is possible!

That feeling that we are all sharing here tonight is the teaching, is the example, of what Fidel and Chávez asked of us.

Sisters and brothers:

As I participated in this event, I was thinking about the road that has brought us this far, and I also remembered a similar event five years ago at the Riverside Church, when we attended, as on this occasion, with the Cuban delegation that was going to participate in a session of the United Nations General Assembly. That night we arrived in Riverside with much nervousness—the spirit of Fidel was there. Fidel visited Riverside and was received by the American community in Riverside; there he explained to the American people the essence of the Cuban Revolution. All that history that we had known since we were children put a lot of pressure on us to be in the same place where Fidel had spoken to the Americans.

That night President Maduro also arrived in Riverside, and that night Riverside, Cuba, and Venezuela received the warmth, the support, the affection, the love, and the solidarity of the American people. The magic and the significance of the place immediately became common, because we were attended with great kindness and love by Gail Walker, present here today. There I met her personally and a friendship and sisterhood began that prevails and will always prevail, right, Gail?

Later, young journalists who work in my team introduced me to Manolo [De Los Santos], a restless young Dominican, a great friend of Cuba, and from the first meeting we talked about socialism, the challenges of socialist construction in such difficult times, and the aspiration for socialism of many young people in the United States who are present here today.

As time went by, Manolo introduced me to Vijay Prashad and with him we also had a conversation of great conviction, of coincidences of ideas, of how to build socialism, of how to promote the ideas of socialism among the youth. We even talked about boxing, and a friendship began which we have shared at various times.

Subsequently, Manolo took a group of young Americans to Cuba—many are present here, our friends, our brothers and sisters from The People's Forum—so we went on several occasions having meetings, talking with them visiting Cuba. We appreciated their support campaigns and how the most just ideas were present in the new generation of Americans. We will never forget the actions you took in solidarity with Cuba when they wanted to isolate us at the Summit of the Americas. We will never forget the demonstrations you have been holding over the years, especially on weekends, against the blockade. And that is why we are here today!

This is the last night we will be in New York during this visit. We visited the headquarters of The People's Forum during these past days, and we were able to talk with Manolo and with others of you. Yesterday, you were demonstrating in the streets of New York—we could not contain ourselves and we had to go to the corner where you were supporting us to greet you, hug you, and thank you.

But what we could not imagine was that in the last hours we were going to be in New York we would be experiencing these emotions in a solidarity event with Venezuela and Cuba. You have given us love, you have given us support, you have given us solidarity. You have embraced us, and we come here today to give you love, to express our solidarity, and to thank you for those embraces. Tonight, at this moment, we are embracing you on behalf of the Cuban people. This meeting fulfills the emotions that we have been experiencing in these days.

The first day of our stay in New York we visited the Malcolm X and Dr. Betty Shabazz Memorial and Educational Center. We went to pay tribute to an American fighter, a defender of human rights, a defender of the African-American people, a defender of just causes. And with this visit we paid tribute to him precisely on the eve of the day on which we commemorated sixty-three years since Malcolm X and Fidel Castro met here in New York. It was September 1960, the State Department had prevented Fidel from staying, and it did not provide the necessary assurances for the Cuban delegation to stay in New York when they were attending a session of the United Nations. And Malcolm X opened the door to Harlem and arranged for Fidel to stay at the Hotel Theresa in Harlem. There began an indestructible friendship, which is also the foundation of the one we are sharing today between the American people and the Cuban people.

During these past days we have been able to have meetings with representatives of different sectors of the American people; with the sectors of science, culture, health; with American businessmen and Cuban businessmen who live in the United States and promote commercial ties with Cuba. We had an intimate meeting with Cubans living in the United States and from them we received messages of support and solidarity, because all of them and you are building bridges of love, like Carlos Lazo, between the Cuban people and the American people.

You will understand that at a time when Cuba is living under an intensified blockade, and when we also feel the effects of this intensification by having been included in a list of countries that supposedly support terrorism, to find ourselves with this support, with this strength, with this encouragement, and with this energy that you are giving us, obliges us to express these feelings and to thank you.

As you know, we have been participating as part of a Cuban delegation in the 78th Session of the United Nations General Assembly. We have come here not only to raise the voice of the Cuban people. We have also come to raise the voice of the peoples of the South, because Cuba is currently chairing the Group of 77 and China, a group of more than 133 nations of the South that coordinates actions in favor of developing countries, a diverse group made up mainly of nations from Africa, Asia, and Latin America and the Caribbean, and in that group we are the South!

We are heirs to a common past as colonies. We suffered the exploitation and plundering of our natural and human resources from which the former European metropolises benefited and enriched themselves. And in contemporary times our peoples have also been victims of expressions of neocolonialism. We are more than 80 percent of the world's population and we are the majority of the people who have been hit hardest by poverty, hunger, misery, deaths from curable diseases, illiteracy, human displacement, and other consequences of underdevelopment. We are also the nations that suffer most from the consequences of climate change, from the climate crisis that the world is experiencing, which is caused by unsustainable production and consumption patterns of capitalism. In short, we are the first and foremost victims of climate change. Cuba insisted that during our *pro tempore* presidency [of the Group of 77 and China] we would promote our commitment to defend the cause of those peoples, which is also the cause of the Cuban people, and it is the cause in favor of the justice that developed countries fight for and which you defend here in the United States.

Today there is an international economic order that generates and perpetuates underdevelopment, that guarantees lucrative and unsustainable lifestyles for only a few minorities, at the expense of depressed living conditions for the majorities in both developing and developed countries. There is a lack of decent jobs, basic quality education systems, health services accessible to all, and other forms of social justice to which all people should have access, to which all the peoples of the world should have access, and which today are not available to large majorities, even in rich countries. That is why we demand solidarity and not selfishness; cooperation and not rivalry; decent work and not exploitation; harmony, respect, and tolerance, and not racism or discrimination of any kind. The peoples have the right to determine their destiny without foreign interference or impositions. Nations have rights over their sources of wealth and their natural resources, which cannot continue to be the untouchable patrimony of large transnational corporations.

Our peoples also have the right to identify and reject the alienating cultural patterns that they try to impose on us, that the media tries to impose on us, which are also new forms of colonization. They aim to demobilize, confuse, disorient, and depress the capacity of mobilization and response of our peoples, promoting selfishness and consumerism, generating apathy and resentment, and at the same time celebrating patterns of success and well-being that are unsustainable. They despise social justice and the value of ideas. They pretend that we ignore our history and try to divide us.

We live in an increasingly polarized world, where spending on armaments is enormous, where production and consumption patterns threaten environmental stability and can lead to pessimism. But that is not the nature of revolutionaries, that is not an option for those of us who believe that a better world is possible, and for those of us who have the conviction that it's worth fighting for that better world that is also possible!

That is why it is a source of great satisfaction for us to meet with you who are comrades, friends, sisters, and brothers who share these ideas. It is a privilege to be able to express on a stage such as this one our gratitude and recognition to those who for so many years have accompanied Cuba's cause in defense of its independence, of the right to determine its own destiny, and to those who for so long have fought against the criminal Yankee blockade.

It is also a privilege to be able to join our voice tonight with yours in solidarity with Venezuela, with Nicaragua, and with the people of Puerto Rico who today celebrate their glorious Grito de Lares! [*exclamations of* "Viva Puerto Rico libre!"] And also with the peoples of Latin America, the Caribbean, Africa, Asia, and all those, even in Europe and North America, who are victims of injustice and inequality. It is also a privilege to share with so many friends and hear in their own voices the political and social problems they face on a daily basis.

In Cuba, the transformative revolutionary process continues on the path of socialism. We are going through particularly difficult times in the management of the economy, as you know, as a consequence of the tightening of the blockade, the effects caused by our inclusion on the list of countries that allegedly support terrorism, and also due to internal problems and shortcomings that we have to overcome; and our friends should know this and we share it with you. You perceive these realities when you visit our country.

The combined effect of the COVID-19 pandemic and the reinforcement of the economic blockade pose significant obstacles to ensuring economic growth and guaranteeing many of the needs of the population. But, even under these conditions, we have not and will not stop prioritizing social justice. We will not stop guaranteeing the fundamental needs of the population. We will continue to defend equity and we will remain committed to the will to protect the socialist system for which so many generations of Cubans have sacrificed. We have never abandoned nor will we ever abandon the principle of solidarity even in times of the greatest material limitations, and we will continue to share not what we have left over but what we have.

As you know, during COVID-19 the United States government acted perversely towards Cuba and behaved criminally in some of the actions it took against our people in those difficult circumstances. It pressured companies in the Latin American and Caribbean region from selling medical oxygen to Cuba when our plant suffered a breakdown in the middle of the pandemic peak. It prevented companies that commercialize pulmonary ventilators from selling them to Cuba when we needed to expand the intensive care units—but our public health system and our scientific level allowed us to overcome adversity.

Cuban scientists, among them young people, created the vaccines that saved the country! Young scientists designed and built high-performance pulmonary ventilators, and thus our disease control ranks among the best in the world, with vaccines, medicines, equipment, and protocols made in Cuba. But it was also very important and highly stimulating for us to receive, in this complex scenario, international solidarity aid, particularly large quantities of syringes that arrived from many parts of the world, including from the United States, which you sent!

Imperialism's gamble in the most difficult hours of these last years has been to bring about the end of the Revolution and the collapse of socialism in Cuba, and it is true that they have caused us damage, hardship, shortages, and other difficulties, but they did not succeed in bringing down the Cuban Revolution, nor will they ever succeed! The creative resistance of the Cuban people has demonstrated that imperialism has no capacity to bend our will, nor to break the commitment of our people to the Revolution and socialism. We have faith in our cause, we are confident in our work for social justice and we feel the solidarity of our brothers and sisters in all parts of the world.

Receive a fraternal and supportive embrace from the people of Cuba! Receive a message of friendship for the American people, and also for all the peoples represented by you here! We firmly believe, as Fidel taught us, "that there is no force in the world capable of crushing the force of truth and ideas."

We will continue together with you fighting for Cuba! Fighting for socialism! Fighting for social justice! Fighting to conquer a better world! And we will succeed! And we will win! And we will win!

Hasta la victoria siempre!

BIOGRAPHIES

Leticia Martínez Hernández

Born in 1984 in Santa Clara, Cuba, she graduated in Journalism from the Marta Abreu de Las Villas Central University. She was a journalist for the *Granma* newspaper and head of its National Editorial Office. She was a correspondent in Haiti during the tragedy caused by the earthquake of January 2010 and was author of the book *El infierno de este mundo, terremoto en Haití.* She has won several journalism awards in Cuba, including the 26 de Julio National Contest, which she won twice, and the Juan Gualberto Gómez Award for the Work of the Year. She was part of the team of journalists that accompanied Army General Raúl Castro Ruz during his term as president of the country. She is currently head of the Communication and Analysis Team of the Presidency of the Republic.

Miguel Díaz-Canel Bermúdez

First Secretary of the Central Committee of the Communist Party of Cuba and President of the Republic of Cuba.

Born on April 20, 1960, in Santa Clara, Cuba he was a successful student and held numerous leadership roles in organizations like the Pioneers Organization, the Federation of Middle School Students (FEEM), and the Federation of University Students (FEU). As a member of the Young Communist League (UJC), he served in various capacities, including First Secretary of the UJC Committee of the Central University of Villa Clara. After earning an Electronic Engineering degree and a master's in Management, he continued to rise through the ranks, serving as First and Second Secretary of the Provincial Committee of the UJC, and eventually transitioning into the Communist Party of Cuba (PCC). In 1994, he became the First Secretary of Villa Clara, earning recognition for his effective leadership. In 2003, he was appointed First Secretary of the PCC in Holguín and elected into the Political Bureau. He served as Minister of Higher Education in 2009, Vice President of the Council of Ministers in 2012, and First Vice President of the Councils of State and Ministers in 2013. His internationalist work in Nicaragua from 1987–1989, along with his advanced education in World Economy and National Defense, and his military service, underscore his comprehensive skills and dedication. His recognitions include the Vanguard of the FEU, Distinguished Service of the FAR, and the Félix Elmusa Order. In 2019, he was elected President of the Republic of Cuba and was reelected to a second term in 2023. As of 2021, he serves as First Secretary of the Communist Party of Cuba.

www.ingramcontent.com/pod-product-compliance
Lightning Source LLC
Chambersburg PA
CBHW020608030426
42337CB00013B/1279